Rousseau

**Rousseau**

Plan For A Constitution For Corsica

Rousseau

**Rousseau**
*Plan For A Constitution For Corsica*

ISBN/EAN: 9783337816360

Printed in Europe, USA, Canada, Australia, Japan

Cover: Foto ©Andreas Hilbeck / pixelio.de

More available books at **www.hansebooks.com**

# Rousseau
## *Project for Corsica*

# PLAN FOR A CONSTITUTION FOR CORSICA

# Plan for a Constitution for Corsica

## Foreword

You are asking for a Plan of a Government good for Corsica. That is asking for more than you think. There are peoples who, however one sets about it, cannot be well governed because the law lacks any hold over them and because a government without law cannot be a good government. On the contrary, the Corsican people, appears to me most fortunately disposed by nature to receive a good administration. But that is not enough. All things can be abused, often necessarily so, and the abuses of political establishments are so closely related to their foundation that it is almost not worth the effort to make one only in order to see it degenerate so quickly.

Some want to ward off this drawback by mechanisms that maintain the government in its primitive condition, they give it a thousand chains, a thousand shackles to keep it in its path, and they encumber it so much that, sagging under the weight of its irons, it remains inactive, immobile, and if it does not decline toward its fall, it does not go toward its end either.

All that comes from separating two inseparable things, namely the body which governs and the body which is governed. By the primitive foundation these two bodies make up only one, they become separated only by the abuse of the foundation.

In such a case, the wisest people, observing relations of suitability, form the government for the nation. Nevertheless, there is something much better to do, that is to form the nation for the government. In the first case, to the extent that the government declines while the nation stays the same, the conformity vanishes; in the second, everything changes at an even pace and the nation, dragging the government along by its force, maintains it when it maintains itself and makes it decline when it declines. The one is always suited to the other.

The Corsican people is in the fortunate condition that makes a good foundation possible; it can depart from the first point and take measures in order not to degenerate. Full of vigor and health it can devote itself to the government that keeps it vigorous and healthy. Nevertheless this establishment must already find some obstacles. The Corsicans have not yet taken on the vices of other nations, but they have already taken on their prejudices; it is these prejudices that must be combated and destroyed in order to form a good establishment.

## [Plan]

The[1] advantageous situation of the island of Corsica and the fortunate natural disposition of its inhabitants seem to offer them a reasonable hope of being able to become a flourishing people and one day to make a figure in Europe if, in the foundation they are meditating they turn their sights in that direction, but the extreme exhaustion into which forty years of continuous war have cast them, the present poverty of their Island and the state of depopulation and devastation it is in does not allow them to give themselves right away the sort of expensive administration that would be needed to give them a public order for that purpose. Moreover, a thousand invincible obstacles would oppose the execution of this plan. Genoa, still mistress of a part of the coast and of almost all the maritime positions, would a thousand times crush their nascent navy ceaselessly exposed to the double danger of the Genoese and the Barbary pirates.[2] They could hold the sea only with armed ships that would cost them ten times more than trade could return to them. Exposed on land and sea, forced to protect themselves on all sides, what would become of them? At everyone's discretion, in their weakness not able to make any advantageous commercial treaty, they would receive the law from everyone; in the midst of so many risks they would have only those profits that no one else would condescend to make, and which would be reduced to nothing. If they overcame all these difficulties by an almost incomprehensible good fortune, their very prosperity, attracting their neighbors' eyes to them, would be a new peril for their poorly established freedom. A constant object of covetousness for the great powers and of jealousy for the small ones, their Island would be threatened at every moment by a new servitude from which it could not extract itself again.

Whatever the Corsican nation's intention might be in giving itself a public order, the first thing it ought to do is to make itself as consistent as it can be by itself. Anyone who depends on someone else and does not have his resources in himself cannot be free. Alliances, treaties, the faith of men, all these can bind the weak to the strong and never bind the strong to the weak. Thus leave negotiations to the powers and do not count on anything but yourself. Brave Corsicans, who knows better than you do everything that one can draw from oneself? Without friends, without support, without money, without an army, enslaved to terrible masters, alone you have thrown off their yoke. You have seen them band together against you, one by one, the most formidable potentates of Europe, flood your Island with foreign armies; you have surmounted everything. Your constancy alone has done what money could never have done; if you wanted to preserve your wealth you would have lost your freedom. You must not draw conclusions from other nations to fit yours. Maxims drawn from your own experience are the best upon which you can govern yourself.

It is less a question of becoming different than you are than of knowing how to preserve yourself that way. Corsicans have gained much since they have been free, they have joined prudence to courage, they have learned to obey their equals, they have acquired virtues and morals, and they do not have any laws at all. If they could stay that way by themselves, I would see almost nothing to do. But when the peril that has brought them together goes away, the factions that it pushes aside will be reborn among them and, instead of bringing their forces together for the maintenance of their independence; they will use them up against each other and will no longer have any for self-defense if someone comes again to attack them. That is what must be forestalled. The divisions among the Corsicans have always been an artifice of their masters for making them weak and dependent; but employed ceaselessly, this artifice has finally produced the inclination and has made them naturally restless, turbulent, hard to govern even by their own leaders. Good laws are necessary, a new foundation is necessary in order to reestablish harmony the very desire for which Tyranny has destroyed. Subjected to foreign masters whose harsh yoke she never bore patiently, Corsica was always turbulent. It is now necessary for her people to study something new; and look for peace in freedom.

Here then are the principles which, according to me, ought to serve as the basis of their legislation: to make use of their people and of their country as much as possible; to cultivate and gather together their own forces, to depend upon them alone, and to think about foreign powers no more than one would if none of them existed.

Let us begin from there to establish the maxims of our foundation.

Being unable to get richer in money, the Island of Corsica ought to try to get richer in men.[3] The power that comes from the population is more real than the one that comes from finances and produces its effect more certainly. Not being able to hide itself, the use of men's arms always reaches the public destination, it is not the same for the use of money; it slips away and melts into private destinations; one heaps it up for one purpose, one gives it out for another; the people pay in order to be protected and what they give serves to oppress them. That is why a state rich in money is always weak, and a state rich in men is always strong.*

In order to multiply men it is necessary to multiply their means of existence, hence agriculture. By this word I do not understand the art of talking about agriculture in a sophisticated way, of establishing academies that speak about it, of writing books that treat it. I do understand a constitution that leads a people to spread itself out over the whole surface of its territory, to settle there, to cultivate all its places, to love the country life, the labors that relate to it, to find the necessities and embellishments of life so well in them that it does not at all desire to leave it.

The taste for agriculture is advantageous to the population not only by multiplying men's means of existence, but also by giving the body of the nation a temperament and morals that cause them to be born in greater number. In every country the inhabitants of the countryside multiply more than those of the cities, either from the simplicity of the rustic life which forms better constituted bodies, or by the constant attention to labor which forestalls disorder and vices. For, everything being equal, the most chaste women, those whose senses are less inflamed by habituation to pleasure, have more children than the others, and it is no less certain that men enervated by debauchery, the certain fruit of idleness, are less fit for generation than those whom a laborious condition makes more temperate.

Peasants are much more attached to their soil than city dwellers are to their towns. For those who do not know any other life, the equality, the simplicity of the rustic one has an attraction that gives them no desire to change it. Hence the satisfaction with one's station which makes man peaceful, hence the love of the fatherland which attaches him to its constitution.

The culture of the earth forms patient and robust men such as they must be to become good soldiers. Those that are taken from the towns are rebellious and soft, they cannot bear the fatigues of war, they fade away in the marches, maladies consume them, they fight among themselves and flee before the enemy. Trained militiamen are the most reliable and best troops; the genuine education of the soldier is to be a plowman.

---

* The majority of usurpers have used one of these two means in order to strengthen their power. The first to impoverish the subjugated peoples and make them barbarians, the other on the contrary to effeminate them under the pretext of educating and enriching them. The first of these ways has constantly produced an effect opposed to its object, and acts of vigor, revolutions, republics on the part of the oppressed peoples have always resulted from them. The other way always succeeds, and softened, corrupt, delicate, reasoning peoples, making fine speeches about freedom in the ignominy of servitude, have all been crushed under their masters then destroyed by conquerors.

The only means for maintaining a State in independence of others is agriculture. Even if you have all the wealth in the world, if you do not have anything with which to nourish yourself you are dependent on others. Your neighbors can give your money whatever value they please because they can wait; but the bread that we need has an indisputable value for us and in every sort of commerce it is always the least hurried person who gives the law to the other. I admit that in a system of finance, it would be necessary to operate in accordance with other views; everything depends on the final aim to which one inclines. Commerce produces wealth but agriculture assures freedom.

It will be said that it would be better to have both at the same time, but they are incompatible as will be shown below. In every country, it will be added, they cultivate the land. I agree to this; just as there is some commerce in every country, in every one they traffic a little or a great deal, but this is not to say that agriculture and commerce flourish everywhere. I am not examining here what is done by the necessity of things but what results from the sort of Government and the general spirit of the nation.

Although the form of Government that a people gives itself might be the work of chance and fortune more often than it is a true choice, nevertheless, there are qualities in the nature and the soil of each country that make one government more suitable than another, and each form of Government has a particular force that brings peoples toward one occupation or another.

The form of Government we have to choose is, on the one hand, the least costly because Corsica is poor, and on the other the most favorable to agriculture because agriculture is at present the sole occupation that can preserve for the Corsican people the independence that it has acquired and give it the consistency it needs.

The least costly administration is the one that passes through the fewest ranks and requires the fewest different orders; such is in general the republican and in particular the democratic state.

The administration most favorable for agriculture is the one whose force, not being at all united in some point, does not involve the unequal distribution of the people, but leaves it evenly dispersed over the territory; such is democracy.

In Switzerland one sees a very striking application of these principles. In general Switzerland is a poor and sterile country. Its government is Republican everywhere. But in cantons that are more fertile than the others such as those of Berne, of Soleure, and of Fribourg, the Government is Aristocratic. In the poorest ones, in those in which cultivation is more unprofitable and requires greater labor the Government is Democratic. The State has only what it needs to continue to exist under the simplest administration. It would exhaust itself and perish under every other one.

It will be said that Corsica, more fertile and in a milder climate, can bear a more burdensome Government. That would be true at another time, but now, crushed by a long enslavement, devastated by long wars, the nation needs to reestablish itself first. When it has developed its fertile soil it will be able to dream about becoming flourishing and giving itself a more brilliant administration. I will say more. The success of the first foundation will make change necessary afterwards. Cultivation of fields cultivates the mind; every people of cultivators multiplies; it multiplies in proportion to the product of its land and if this land is fecund it finally multiplies so strongly that the land is no longer sufficient for it; then it is forced to establish colonies or to change its government.

When the country is saturated with inhabitants one can no longer use the surplus for cultivation. Then this surplus must be employed in industry, in commerce, in the Arts and this new system requires a different administration. May the establishment that Corsica is going to make soon make it necessary for it to change this way. But as long as it does not have more men than it can nourish, as long as an inch of land lying fallow remains on the Island, it ought to hold to the rustic system and change it only when the Island is not sufficient for it.

As I have said the rustic system entails the Democratic state. Thus the form that we have to choose is given. It is true that there are some modifications to make in its application because of the size of the Island; for a purely democratic government suits a small town rather than a nation. One could not assemble the whole people of a country like that of a city and when the supreme authority is conferred upon deputies, the government changes and becomes Aristocratic. The one that suits Corsica is a mixed Government in which the people is assembled only in parts and in which the depositaries of its power are often changed. This was seen very well by the author of the memorandum written in 1764 at Vescovado, an excellent memorandum, which one can consult confidently about everything that is not explained in this one.[4]

If it is well established, two great advantages will result from this form. One, to confer the administration only upon a small number, which allows the selection of enlightened people. The other, to make all the members of the State collaborate in the supreme authority, which, making all the people perfectly level, allows it to spread out over the whole surface of the Island and to populate it evenly everywhere. This is the fundamental maxim of our foundation. Let us make it so that it keeps its population in equilibrium everywhere and by that alone we will have made it as perfect as it could be. If this maxim is good, our rules become clear and our work is simplified to a surprising extent.

A part of this work has already been done: we have fewer establishments than prejudices to destroy, it is less a question of changing than of completing. The Genoese themselves prepared your foundation and with a care worthy of Providence they founded freedom while believing they were consolidating Tyranny. They deprived you of almost all commerce and now is not in fact the time to have any. If it were open abroad it would be necessary to forbid it until your constitution has found its footing and until the interior furnished you with everything you can draw from it. They have hindered the exportation of your commodities. It is not at all to your advantage to export them, but rather that enough men be born on the Island to consume them.

The counties[5] and particular jurisdictions they formed or preserved in order to facilitate the collection of taxes and the execution of orders are the only possible way to establish democracy in a whole people which cannot assemble at the same time in the same place; they are also the only means of keeping the country independent of the cities which are easier to keep under the yoke. They also applied themselves to destroying the nobility, to depriving it of its functions, of its titles, extinguishing the great fiefs; it is fortunate for you that they took upon themselves what was odious in this enterprise and which you perhaps would not have been able to do if they had not done it before you. Do not hesitate at all to complete their work; while believing they were working for themselves, they were working for you. Only the goal is very different, for the goal of the Genoese was in the thing itself and yours is in its effect. They wanted only to debase the nobility and you want to ennoble the nation.[6]

This is a point on which I see that the Corsicans do not yet have healthy ideas. In all their documentary memoranda, in their protestation of Aix-la-Chapelle they complained that Genoa weakened or rather destroyed their nobility.[7] That was a doubtless a grievance, but this was not a misfortune, on the contrary it is an advantage, without which it would be impossible for them to remain free.

To put the dignity of a State in the titles of some of its members is to take the shadow for the body. When the Kingdom of Corsica belonged to Genoa it might have been useful to it to have marquises, counts, titled nobles who served so to speak as mediators between the Corsican people and the Republic. But now against whom would such protectors be useful to it, protectors less suited to protecting it from Tyranny than to usurping it themselves, who would lay it waste by their quarrels and their disputes, until one of them, having enslaved the others, made all his fellow citizens into his subjects?

Let us distinguish two sorts of nobility. Feudal nobility, which is connected with Monarchy, and political nobility, which is connected with Aristocracy. The first has numerous orders or degrees, some titled, others not titled, from great vassals to simple Gentlemen; its rights, although hereditary, are so to speak individual, private, attached to each family and so independent of each other that they are even independent of the constitution of the state and of sovereignty. The second, on the contrary, united into a single indivisible body all of whose rights are in the body and not in its members, forms so essential a part of the body politic that the former cannot continue to exist without the latter nor the latter without the former, and all the individuals who compose it, equal by their birth in titles, in privileges, in authority, merge under the shared name of patricians.

It is clear from the titles that the ancient Corsican nobility bore and from the fiefs that it possessed, with rights approaching sovereignty itself, that it was in the first class and that it owed its origin either to Moorish or French conquerors, or to Princes in whom the Popes had vested the Island of Corsica. Now this sort of nobility can so little enter into a democratic or mixed Republic that it cannot even enter into an aristocracy, for aristocracy accepts only corporate rights and not individual rights. Democracy does not know any nobility other than virtue except for freedom, and, in the same way, aristocracy does not know any nobility other than authority. Everything foreign to the constitution ought to be carefully banished from the body politic. Thus, leave to other states all those titles of Marquis and of Count, debasing for simple Citizens. The fundamental law of your foundation ought to be equality. Everything ought to be related to it, even authority itself which is established only to defend it. All ought to be equal by right of birth. The state ought not to grant distinctions except to merit, to virtues, to services rendered to the fatherland and these distinctions ought not to be any more hereditary than are the qualities based on which they are founded. We shall soon see how one can calibrate different orders in a people without birth and nobility entering into it for anything.

All fiefs, homages, rents, and feudal rights hitherto abolished will therefore be so forever, and the state will buy back those that still continue to exist so that all seigniorial rights will remain extinct and suppressed on the whole Island.

So that all the parts of the State might keep among themselves, as much as possible, the same levelness that we are trying to establish among the individuals, the limits of the districts, counties, and jurisdictions will be regulated in such a manner as to diminish the extreme inequality that makes itself felt there. The province of Bastia and Nebbio alone contains as many inhabitants as the seven provinces of Capo Corso, Alleria, Porto Vecchio, Sartene, Vico, Calvi, and Algagliola. That of Ajaccio contains more than the four adjacent to it. Without removing the boundaries entirely and overturning the jurisdictions, one can moderate these enormous disproportions by means of some slight changes. For example the abolition of fiefs makes it easy to form out of those of Canari, Brando, and Nonza, a new jurisdiction which, strengthened by the County of Pietrabugno, will be found to be just about equal to the jurisdiction of Capo Corso. The fief of Istria joined to the Province of Sartene will still not make it equal to that of Corte, and that of Bastia and Nebbio, even though diminished by one County, can be divided into two still very strong jurisdictions which will be separated by the Guolo. This is only an example for making myself understood; for I do not know the locale well enough to be able to settle anything.

By these slight changes the Island of Corsica, which I am assuming to be entirely free, would be found to be divided into twelve jurisdictions which will not be extremely disproportionate, above all when, the municipal rights of the cities having been restricted as they ought to be, less weight will remain in the jurisdiction of these cities.

Cities are useful in a country in the proportion to the cultivation of commerce and the arts there, but they are harmful to the system that we have adopted. Their inhabitants are cultivators or idle. Now cultivation is always done better by settlers than by city-dwellers, and all the vices that have devastated Corsica up to this moment come from idleness. The stupid pride of bourgeois does nothing but debase and discourage the plowman. Given over to softness, to the passions it excites, they plunge into debauchery and sell themselves in order to satisfy it; self-interest makes them servile and laziness makes them restless, they are slaves or rebels, never free. This difference made itself felt very much throughout all of the present war, and since the nation has broken its irons. It is the vigor of your counties that brought about the revolution, it is their firmness that sustained it; that unbreakable courage that no reversal can beat down comes to you from them. Cities populated by mercenary men have sold their nation in order to preserve for themselves some petty privileges that the Genoese know artfully to turn to good account and, justly punished for their cowardice, they remain nests of Tyranny, while already the Corsican people are gloriously enjoying the freedom that it acquired at the price of its blood.

A cultivating people must not look covetously at residence in cities and envy the fate of the sluggards who live there; consequently the habitation of cities must not be favored at all by advantages harmful to the general population and to the freedom of the nation. A plowman must not be inferior by birth to anyone, he must see above him only the laws and the magistrates and he must be capable of becoming a magistrate himself if he is worthy of it from his enlightenment or from his probity. In a word, the cities and their inhabitants, no more than the fiefs and their possessions, ought to keep any exclusive privilege; the whole Island ought to enjoy the same rights, bear the same expenses, and become without distinction what is called in the terms of the country: *terra di commune.*[8]

Now if cities are harmful, capitals are even more so. A capital is a pit into which almost the entire nation goes to lose its morals, its laws, its courage, and its freedom. It is imagined that big cities favor agriculture because they consume a great deal of commodities, but they consume even more cultivators, either from the desire of taking on a better profession which attracts them or from the natural wasting away of bourgeois races which the countryside always brings up to strength. The surroundings of capitals have an air of life, but the farther one goes from them the more deserted everything is. From the capital is exhaled a continuous plague which undermines and finally destroys the nation.

Nevertheless, the Government must have a center, a meeting point to which everything is related: there would be too much inconvenience in having the supreme administration roam. In order to make it circulate from Province to Province it would be necessary to divide the Island into several small confederated States each one of which would have the Presidency in its turn; but this system would complicate the action of the machine, its pieces would be less tied together. Not big enough to make this division necessary, the Island is too big to be able to do without a capital. But this capital must bring about the correspondence of all the jurisdictions without attracting their people; everything must be connected to it and each thing must stay in its place. In a word the seat of the supreme Government must be less a capital than an administrative center.

On this issue, necessity by itself has directed the nation's selection just as reason itself would have done. Having remained masters of the maritime positions, the Genoese have left you only the city of Corte, not any less fortunately situated for the Corsican administration than Bastia was for the Genoese administration. Positioned in the middle of the Island, Corte sees all its shores at almost equal distances. It is precisely between the two great parts *di quà e di là da'i monti*[9] equally within reach of all. It is far from the sea which will preserve the morals, the simplicity, the uprightness, the national character of its inhabitants for longer than if it were subject to the influx of foreigners. It is in the most elevated part of the Island, in very healthy air, but in an unfertile soil, and being almost at the source of the rivers, which, at first making accessibility of supplies more difficult, does not allow it to grow too much. If one adds to all that the precaution of not making any of the great functions the State hereditary or even for life, it is to be presumed that the public men, having only temporary occupancy there, will not give it that fatal splendor that causes the luster and the ruin of States for a long time.

These are the first reflections that a rapid examination of the site of the Island has suggested to me. Before speaking in more detail about the Government, now it is necessary to begin by seeing what it ought to do and upon what maxims it ought to be conducted. That is what ought to conclude the decision about its form, for each form of Government has its spirit which is natural, proper to it, and from which it will never diverge.[10]

Up to now we have distributed the national soil as equally as we could; now let us seek to draw the plan of the building that is to be built there. The first rule we have to follow is the national character. Every people has or ought to have a national character, and if it lacks one it would be necessary to begin by giving it one. Islanders above all, being less mixed, less blended with other peoples, ordinarily have a more marked one. The Corsicans in particular have a naturally very perceptible one; and if being so disfigured by slavery and Tyranny it has become difficult to know, on the other hand it is also easy to reestablish and preserve because of its isolated position.

The Island of Corsica, says Diodorus, is mountainous, full of woods, and watered by large rivers. Its inhabitants feed themselves upon milk, honey, and meat with which the country generously furnishes them. They observe among themselves the rules of justice and humanity more precisely than the other barbarians; the one who first finds some honey on the mountains and in hollows of trees is assured that no one will dispute it with him. They are always certain of finding their sheep upon which each puts his mark and which they afterwards allow to graze in the countryside without anyone watching over them: the same spirit of equity appears to guide them in all the encounters of life.[11]

In the simplest narratives and without reasoning themselves, the great historians know how to make perceptible to the reader the reason for every fact they report.

When a country is not populated by colonies, it is from the nature of the soil that the primitive character of the inhabitants is born. A rough, uneven terrain, hard to cultivate, ought to furnish more nourishment for animals than for men, fields must be rare there and pastures abundant. From that comes the multiplication of livestock and pastoral life. The flocks of private individuals wandering in the mountains mix together there, blend. Honey has no key other than the mark of the first occupier; property cannot be established or preserved except through public faith and it is very necessary for everyone to be just, otherwise no one would have anything and the nation would perish.

Mountains, woods, rivers, pastures. Would one not believe that one was reading the description of Switzerland? Also was the same character that Diodorus attributes to the Corsicans not found in the Swiss: equity, humanity, good faith? The whole difference was that, living in a rougher climate they were more laborious. Buried under the snow for six months, they were forced to make provisions for the winter, scattered over their rocks, they cultivated them with a fatigue that made them robust; a continuous labor deprived them of the time to become acquainted with the passions; communication was always difficult, when the snow and ice finished closing them up, each was forced to suffice for himself and his family in his hut: from that came fortunate and unpolished industry. Each practiced all the necessary arts in his house; all were masons, carpenters, joiners, wheelwrights. On the other hand, the rivers and the torrents that separated them from each other gave each the means of doing without his neighbors. With saws, forges, mills multiplying, they learned to arrange the streams of water both for the operation of wheels and for distributing the water to many places. This is how, each, living on his land in the midst of their precipices and their vales, succeeded in drawing all he needed from it, in living on a generous scale there, in desiring nothing outside. With interests and needs that did not intersect at all and none of them dependent on anyone else, the only relations they had among themselves were relations of benevolence and friendship; harmony and peace reigned effortlessly in their large families, they had almost nothing else to deal with among themselves except marriages in which inclination alone was consulted, which ambition did not form at all, which interest and inequality never stopped. In the most perfect independence, this poor but not needy people multiplied in a union that nothing could corrupt; it did not have any virtues because, not having any vices at all to conquer, doing good cost it nothing, and it was good and just without even knowing what justice and virtue were. From the force with which this laborious and independent life attached the Swiss to their fatherland resulted two greater means for defending it, namely agreement in resolutions and courage in combat. When one considers the constant union that reigned among men without masters, almost without laws, and which the Princes who surrounded them struggled to divide by all the maneuvers of policy; when one sees the unbreakable firmness, the constancy, even the ferocity that these terrible men brought into combat, resolved to die or to conquer and not even having the idea of separating their life from their freedom, one no longer has any difficulty in conceiving the prodigies they performed for the defense of their country and their independence, one is no longer surprised at seeing the three greatest powers and the most warlike troops of Europe fail successively in their undertakings against this heroic nation whose simplicity made it as invincible to ruse as its courage was to valor. Corsicans, here is the model that you ought to follow to return to your primitive state.

But these rustic men, who at first did not know anything but themselves, their mountains, and their livestock, learned to know other nations by defending themselves against them. Their victories opened the borders in their neighborhood to them, their reputation for bravery engendered in Princes the idea of employing them. They began to pay these troops they had been unable to conquer. These brave people who had defended their freedom so well became the oppressors of other people's freedom. It was surprising to see them bring to the service of Princes the same valor they had put into resisting them, the same fidelity they had kept for the fatherland; sell at the price of money the virtues that can least be bought and that money corrupts most quickly. But in these first times they brought to the service of Princes the same pride they had put into resisting them; they looked at themselves less as henchmen than as defenders and believed they had sold them less their services than their protection.

Insensibly they debased themselves and were no longer anything but mercenaries. The taste for money made them feel that they were poor; disdain for their station insensibly destroyed the virtues that were its work and the Swiss became five-penny men, as the French are four-penny ones. Another more hidden cause corrupted this vigorous nation. Their isolated and simple life made them independent as well as robust; each knew no master but himself; but all, having the same interests and the same tastes, united without difficulty in order to want and do the same things; the uniformity of their life took the place of law for them. But when the frequentation of other peoples make them love what they ought to have feared and admire what they ought to have disdained, the ambition of the principal men made them change their maxims; they felt that in order to dominate the people better it was necessary to give them more dependent tastes. From that came the introduction of commerce, of industry, and of luxury, which, tying private individuals to the public authority by their professions and by their needs, made them depend upon those who govern much more than they depended on them in their primitive state.

Poverty did not make itself felt in Switzerland until money began to circulate there. It put the same inequality into resources as in fortunes; for acquiring, it became a great means of which those who had nothing were deprived. Establishments of commerce and manufacturing multiplied. The arts took multitudes of hands away from agriculture. While distributing themselves unevenly, men multiplied, they spread out into countries more favorably situated and where resources were even easier to come by. Some deserted their fatherland, others became useless to it by consuming while not producing anything. The multitude of children became burdensome. Population growth sensibly diminished, and while they multiplied in the cities, since the cultivation of the lands was more neglected and the necessities of life more costly, which made foreign commodities more necessary, they made the country more dependent on its neighbors. The idle life introduced corruption and multiplied pensioners of the powers; love of the fatherland, extinguished in all hearts, gave way there to love of money alone; all the feelings that give resiliency to the soul being stifled, one no longer saw either firmness in conduct or vigor in resolutions. Previously poor Switzerland gave the law to France, now rich Switzerland trembles at the knit brow of a French minister.

These are great lessons for the Corsican people; let us see how it ought to apply them. The Corsican people preserve a large number of its primitive virtues which will facilitate our constitution a great deal. In its servitude it has also contracted many vices which it ought to cure; of these vices some will disappear by themselves along with the cause that gave birth to them, others need a cause to uproot the passion that produced them.[12]*

In the first class I put the indomitable and ferocious mood that is attributed to them. They are accused of being unruly; how is this known since they have never been governed justly? By animating them ceaselessly against each other, it should have been foreseen that this animosity would often turn against those whose work it was.

---

* There is in all states (peoples) a progression, a natural and necessary development from their birth until their destruction. In order to make their duration as long and also as fine as possible, it is better to take note of (to push back) the first limit to before rather than after this point of vigor (and of force) (It is better that the state has still to grow in strength from the moment of institution than no longer to have anything but to decline) One must not wish that Corsica be right away what it can be (for it would not maintain itself at all in such a condition); it is better that it arrive there and that it ascend rather than to be there right away and do nothing but decline. The condition of wasting away in which it is would make its condition of vigor into a very weak condition, instead of which, by disposing it to reach it, this condition will afterwards be a very good condition.

I put in the second class the inclination toward theft and murder which has made them odious. The source of these two vices is laziness and impunity; that is clear as to the first, and easy to prove as to the second since the family hatreds and plans for vengeance with which they were ceaselessly occupied with satisfying are born in idle conversations and take consistency in somber meditations and are executed without difficulty because of the assurance of impunity.

Who could not be seized with horror against a barbarous Government that, in order to see these unfortunate people cutting each other's throats, did not spare any effort for inciting them to do so? Murder was not punished; what am I saying, it was rewarded; the price for blood was one of the republic's revenues; in order to avoid a total destruction it was necessary for the unfortunate Corsicans to buy the favor of being disarmed by means of a tribute.

The Genoese boasted about having favored agriculture on the Island, the Corsicans appear to agree with them. I would not similarly agree; the poor success proves that they had made use of poor means. In this conduct, the Republic did not have as a goal multiplying the inhabitants of the Island, since it so openly favored murders, nor making them live in comfort since it ruined them by exactions, nor even facilitating the collection of taxes since it burdened commodities with duties of sale and transportation and forbade their exportation. On the contrary, it had as its goal making more onerous these same taxes which it did not dare to increase, always holding the Corsicans in abasement by attaching them so to speak to their soil, by turning them away from commerce, the arts, from all the lucrative professions, by keeping them from rising up, from being educated, from becoming rich. Its goal was to get all produce dirt cheap from the monopolies of its officials. It took every measure for draining the Island of money in order to make it necessary there, and in order always to keep it from returning to it. Tyranny could not apply a more refined maneuver, while appearing to favor cultivation, it succeeded in crushing the nation; it wanted to reduce it to a heap of base peasants living in the most deplorable misery.

What happened from that? The discouraged Corsicans abandoned a labor that was not animated by any hope. They preferred to do nothing rather than to fatigue themselves at a pure loss. The laborious and simple life gave way to laziness, to inaction, to all sorts of vices, theft procured them the money they needed to pay their tax, and which they did not find at all with their produce; they left their fields in order to labor as highwaymen.

May the Corsicans, brought back to a laborious life, lose the habit of

wandering around the Island like bandits, may their even and simple oc-
cupations keeping them absorbed in their family leave them few interests
to contest among themselves! May their labor easily furnish them with
enough to continue to exist, them and their family! May those who have
everything necessary for life not also be obliged to have money in cash,
either to pay taxes and other impositions or to furnish needs of whims
and of luxury, which, without contributing to the well-being of the one
who shows it off, only stimulates other people's envy and hatred!

One easily sees how the system to which we have given preference
leads to these advantages, but that is not enough. It is a question of making the people adopt this system's practices, of making it love the occupation we want to give it, of fixing its pleasures, its desires, its tastes there,
in general of making it into the happiness of life, and of limiting plans of
ambition to it.

I see no more prompt and more certain means for reaching that point
than the two following ones: the one of attaching men to the land, so
to speak, by drawing their distinctions and their rights from it, and the
other, of strengthening this bond by that of the family by making the
land necessary to the station of fathers.

In this intention, I thought that, by posing the fundamental law upon
distinctions drawn from the nature of the thing, one could divide the
whole Corsican nation into three classes whose constant personal inequality could happily be substituted for the inequality of descent or habitation
that results from the municipal feudal system that we are abolishing.

The first class will be that of citizens.

The second that of Patriots.

The third that of aspirants.

It will be said below by what titles one will be inscribed in each class
and what privileges one will enjoy there.

This distinction by Classes ought not at all to be done by a census or
enumeration at the moment of foundation, but it ought to be established
gradually by itself by the simple progression of time. The first act of the
planned establishment ought to be a solemn oath sworn by all Corsicans
of twenty years of age and older, and all those who swear this oath ought
to be inscribed without distinction in the number of citizens. It is very
just that all these valiant men who have freed their nation at the price of
their blood enter into possession of all these advantages and enjoy in the
first rank the freedom they acquired for it.

But from the day the union has been formed and the oath solemnly
sworn, all those born on the Island who have not come of age will remain

in the Class of aspirants until they can ascend to the two other classes upon the following conditions.

Every aspirant married in accordance with the law, who has some estate of his own independently of his wife's dowry will be inscribed in the class of the patriots.

Every patriot married or widowed who has two living children, a habitation of his own, and an estate of land sufficient for his subsistence will be inscribed in the class of citizens.

This first step, sufficient for making land esteemed, is not sufficient for putting it into cultivation unless one removes the necessity for money that caused the Island's poverty under the Genoese government. It is necessary to establish as a definite maxim that everywhere that money is of the utmost necessity the nation detaches itself from agriculture in order to throw itself into more lucrative professions; the station of plowman is then either an object of commerce and a sort of manufacture for the big farmers, or the last resource of poverty for the crowd of peasants. When they have earned enough, those who get rich by means of commerce and industry place their money in landed estates which others cultivate for them; the whole nation thus finds itself divided into rich sluggards who possess the land and wretched peasants who do not have enough to live on while cultivating it.

The more necessary money is for private individuals, the more necessary it is for the government; from which it follows that, the more commerce flourishes, the higher the taxes are, and in order to pay these taxes it is useless for the peasant to cultivate his land if he does not sell its product. He might very well have wheat, wine, oil, he absolutely needs money, he must carry his produce here and there into the towns, make himself into a petty merchant, petty salesman, petty knave. Brought up in brokering, his children become debauched, attach themselves to the towns, lose the taste for their station and make themselves into sailors or soldiers rather than take on their father's station. Soon the countryside is depopulated and the town swarms with vagabonds, little by little bread is lacking, public poverty increases along with the opulence of some private individuals and in concert both things bring about all the vices that finally cause the ruin of a nation.

I look at every system of commerce as destructive of agriculture so much so that I make no exception even for commerce in commodities that are the product of agriculture. For it to be maintained in this system, the profit would have to be capable of being divided equally between the merchant and the cultivator. But this is what is impossible because the trade of the one being free and that of the other forced, the first will always give the law to the second, a relation which—breaking equilibrium—cannot form a solid and permanent condition.

It must not be imagined that the Island will be richer when it has a lot of money. This is true in relation to other peoples, and by its external relations, but in itself a nation is neither richer nor poorer for having more or less money or, what comes down to the same thing, because the same quantity of money circulates there more or less actively. Not only is money a sign, but it is a relative sign which has a genuine effect only by the inequality of its distribution. For assuming that on the Island of Corsica each private individual has only ten crowns or that he has one hundred thousand crowns, the respective condition of all is absolutely the same in the two cases; there are neither richer nor poorer among them and the only difference is that the second assumption makes trade more troublesome. If Corsica needed foreigners it would need money, but being able to be self-sufficient, it does not need it; and since it is useful only as a sign of inequality, the less of it that circulates in the Island the more real abundance will reign there.[13]

It is necessary to see whether what is being done with money cannot be done without money; and assuming that it can be, it is necessary to compare the two means relatively to our object.

It is proven by the facts that, even in the fallow and exhausted state in which it is, the Island of Corsica is sufficient for the subsistence of its inhabitants, since for thirty-six years of war when they handled weapons more than the plow, never did, nevertheless, a single ship of produce and provisions of any sort arrive for their use. It even has all that it needs in addition to provisions to put them and maintain them in a flourishing state without borrowing anything from abroad. It has wool for its fabric, hemp and linen for sails and rigging, leather for shoes, timber for the navy, iron for forges, copper for utensils and for small coinage. It has some salt for its use; it will have much more beyond that by reestablishing the saltworks of Alleria which the Genoese kept in a state of destruction with so much difficulty and expense, and which still gave salt in spite of them. Even if they wanted to, the Corsicans could not carry on trade abroad without buying superfluities; thus even in such a case money would not be necessary for them for commerce, since it is the only merchandise that they would go looking for. It follows from this that, in these relations of nation to nation, Corsica has no need of money.

In the interior the Island is rather large and divided by mountains; its large and numerous rivers are hardly navigable; its parts do not naturally communicate among each other; but the difference of their products ties them in a mutual dependence by the need they have for each other. The Province of Capo Corso, which produces almost nothing but wine, needs the wheat and oils that Balagna provides it. On the heights, in the same way Corte yields grains and lacks all the rest; Bonifacio, at the feet of rocks at the other extremity of the Island, needs everything and provides nothing. The project of an evenly distributed population thus requires a circulation of commodities, an easy flowing from one jurisdiction into another and consequently an interior commerce.

But to this I say two things. One, that with the cooperation of the government this commerce can be done in large part by exchanges; the other, that with the same cooperation and from a natural consequence of our establishment, this commerce and these exchanges ought to diminish from day to day and finally be reduced to very little consequence.

It is known that in the exhaustion into which the Genoese had put Corsica, money, always leaving and not returning at all, became so rare in the end that in some cantons of the Island currency was not even known and that they made neither sales nor purchases except by exchanges.

In their memoranda the Corsicans have cited this fact among their grievances; they were right, since, money being necessary for paying the taxes, these poor people who no longer had any, seized and enforced upon their households, saw themselves despoiled of their most necessary utensils, of their furnishings, of their clothing, of their rags which it was necessary to transport from one place to another and the sale of which did not return the tenth part of their value. So that, for lack of money, they paid ten times for one imposition.

But, since in our system one will no longer be forced to pay the tax in specie, the lack of money—not being at all a sign of poverty—will not serve at all for increasing it; exchanges can be made in kind and without intermediate values, and one will be able to live in abundance without ever handling a penny.

I see that under the Genoese governors who forbade and in a thousand ways hindered trade of produce from one province to another, communes made storehouses of wheat, of wine, of oil to wait for the favorable and allowed moment for trade, and that these storehouses served the Genoese officials as pretext for a thousand odious monopolies. Since the idea of these storehouses is not new, it will be all the easier to put it into practice and will provide a convenient and simple means for exchange for the public and for private individuals without risk of the inconveniences that made it onerous to the people.

Even without having recourse to these storehouses or bonded warehouses, one could establish in each parish or county seat a double-entry public register in which each year private individuals would have inscribed on one side the sort and quantity of produce that they have in excess and on the other those that they lack. From the balance and comparison of these registers made from province to province one could regulate the prices of produce and the volume of trade so well that each County would make the consumption of what was superfluous and the acquisition of what was necessary, without there being either deficit or excess in quantity and almost as conveniently as if its harvest was proportioned to its needs.

These operations can be done with the greatest precision and without real money, either by means of exchanges or by aid of a simple ideal money that would serve as expression of comparison as, for example, pistoles are in France, or by taking as money some real good which is numbered as were oxen among the Greeks or sheep among the Romans, and which one settles in its average value, for then an ox can be worth more or less than one ox and a sheep more or less than one sheep, a difference which makes the ideal money preferable, because it is always precise, not being taken for anything but an abstract number.

As long as one sticks to that, trade will be maintained in equilibrium and exchanges, being regulated solely on the relative abundance or rarity of produce and on the greater or lesser ease of transportation, will always and everywhere remain compensated relatively, and all the productions of the Island being dispersed equally will take on the level of the population by themselves. I add that without inconvenience the public administration will be able to preside over this trade, over these exchanges, keeping balance in them, regulating the volume, making their distribution because as long as they are made in kind the public officials will not be able to abuse them and will not even have the temptation to do so; whereas the conversion of produce into money opens the door to all the exactions, to all the monopolies, to all the knavishness usual to people in positions in such cases.

One must expect much confusion at the beginning, but this confusion is inevitable in every establishment that is beginning and is opposed to an established practice. I add that once this rule has been established it will become easier every year not only from practice and experience, but from the successive decrease in trade that should necessarily result from it until it is reduced by itself to the smallest quantity possible, which is the final goal that ought to be proposed.

Everyone must live and no one get rich. This is the fundamental principle of the nation's prosperity, and for its part the public order that I am proposing moves toward this goal as directly as possible.[14]

Not being at all an object of commerce and not yielding any money, the superfluous produce will be cultivated only in proportion to the need that will be had for what is necessary and anyone who can procure for himself immediately the ones he lacks will not have any interest in having too much.

As soon as the products of the earth are not merchandise at all, their cultivation will little by little adjust itself in each province and even in each private holding to the general need of the province and the particular need of the cultivator. Each will exert himself to have everything that he needs in kind and by his own cultivation rather than by means of exchanges that will certainly always be less convenient, however easily they might be made.

Without contradiction it is an advantage for each piece of land to produce what is best suited to it; by this disposition one draws more and more easily from a country than by any other. But this consideration, as important as it is, is only secondary. It would be better for the land to produce a little less and the inhabitants be better ordered. Among all these movements of traffic and exchange it is impossible for destructive vices not to slip into a nation. The lack of some conveniences in the selection of pieces of land can be compensated for by labor and it would be better to use fields badly than men. Moreover, every cultivator can and ought to make this choice in his land and each parish or community in its communal goods, as is said below.

It will be feared, I feel it, that this economy might produce an effect contrary to the one that I expect from it, that instead of stimulating cultivation it might discourage[15] it, that the settlers, having no demand for their produce might neglect their labors, that they might limit themselves to subsistence without seeking abundance, and that satisfied with harvesting what is absolutely necessary for themselves, they might moreover leave their lands fallow.[16] It will even appear well founded based on the experience of the Genoese government under which the prohibition of exporting commodities outside of the Island produced exactly this effect.

But it is necessary to consider that under that administration money, being of primary necessity, formed the immediate object of labor, that consequently all labor that could not produce money was necessarily neglected, that the cultivator weighed down with disdain, vexations, miseries regarded his station as the height of misfortune, that seeing that he could not find his needs in it he sought another one or fell into discouragement. Instead of which, all the intentions of the foundation here tend to make this station happy in its mediocrity, respectable in its simplicity. Furnishing all the needs of life, all the public tributes without sales and without trafficking, all the means for consideration, it will not even allow a better or nobler one to be imagined. Not seeing anything above them, those who carry it on will make it their glory, and opening up for themselves a path to greater employments they will fill it like the first Romans. Not being able to leave this station, one will want to distinguish oneself in it, one will want to fill it better than others do, to make larger harvests, to furnish a stronger contingent to the state, to deserve the people's votes in elections. Large families well nourished and well clothed will bring honor to leaders; and, since real abundance will be the sole object of luxury, each will want to distinguish himself by that sort of luxury. As long as the human heart remains what it is such establishments will not produce laziness.

What the particular magistrates and the fathers of families ought to do in each jurisdiction, in each county, in each private holding in order not to need others, the general government of the Island ought to do in order not to need the neighboring people.

An exact record of the merchandise that has entered the Island during a certain number of years will give a certain and faithful account about the things it cannot do without; for luxury and superfluity cannot occur in the present situation. With attentive observation over both what the Island produces and what it can produce it will be found that the foreign things necessary are reduced to very little. This is confirmed perfectly by the facts, since in the years 1735 and '36 when the Island, blockaded by the Genoese navy, had no communication with the mainland not only was there no lack of foodstuffs, but no unbearable needs of any sort. Those which made themselves felt the most were munitions for war, leather, cottons for wicks; the pith of certain reeds even took the place of this latter.

From this small number of necessary importations it is still necessary to retrench everything that the Island does not furnish now, but which it can furnish when better cultivated and enlivened by industry. The more carefully one ought to set aside the idle arts, the arts of comfort and softness, the more one ought to favor those that are useful for agriculture and advantageous to human life. We do not need either sculptors or goldsmiths, but we do need carpenters and blacksmiths, we do need weavers, good woolworkers, and not embroiderers or drawers of gold.

The beginning will be made by making sure of the most necessary raw materials, namely wood, iron, wool, leather, hemp, and flax. The Island abounds in wood both for building and for heating, but one should not take pride in this abundance and abandon the use and cutting down of forests to the sole discretion of the owners. To the extent that the population of the Island increases and clearing expands, a rapid devastation of the woods will be caused which can be replaced only very slowly. On this point one can draw lessons of foresight from the country in which I live.[17] Switzerland was formerly covered with woods in such abundance that it was inconvenienced by it. But both for the expansion of pasturage and for the establishment of manufacturing they were cut down without measure and without rule; now these immense forests show only almost naked rocks. Fortunately, warned by the example of France, the Swiss have seen the danger and have put as much order into it as they could. It remains to be seen whether their precautions are not too late; for if, in spite of these precautions, their woods are diminishing daily it is clear that they must soon be destroyed.

By setting about it from farther away, Corsica will not have to fear the same danger. It is necessary to establish early a precise public order over the forests and to regulate the cutting so that reproduction equals consumption. It will be necessary not to act as in France, where the masters of water and forests, having a right over the cutting of trees, have an interest in destroying everything, a care which they also discharge as well as they can. It is necessary to foresee the future from afar: although it might not be appropriate to establish a navy at present, the time will come when this establishment must take place and then the advantage of not having given over to foreign navies the fine forests that are close to the sea will be felt. The old woods which are no longer thriving ought to be exploited or sold, but it is necessary to leave standing all those that are in their strength; they will have their time for use.

It is said that a copper mine has been found on the Island; that is good, but iron mines are worth even more. There surely are some on the Island; the situation of the mountains, the nature of the terrain, the thermal waters that one finds in the province of Capo Corso and elsewhere, everything makes me believe that many of these mines will be found if one looks well for them and if one uses capable people in these searches. That being assumed, one will not allow their exploitation indiscriminately, but one will choose the most favorable positions, the ones most within reach of the woods and rivers in order to establish forges, and where one will be able to open routes most convenient for transportation.

One will have the same attention to manufacturing of all sorts, each in the things that concern them, so as to facilitate labor and distribution as much as possible. Nevertheless, one will be very careful not to set up these sorts of establishments in the most populated and most fertile districts of the Island. On the contrary, everything being equal, one will choose the most arid pieces of land which would remain deserted if they were not populated by industry. From that there will be some additional difficulty for the necessary provisioning; but the advantages that will be found there and the inconveniences that will be avoided ought to prevail infinitely over that consideration.

First, this way we are following our great and first principle which is not only to extend and multiply the population but to spread it out evenly over the whole Island as much as possible. For if the sterile places were not populated by industry they would remain deserted and this would be so much lost for the possible enlargement of the nation.

If one set up such establishments in fertile places, the abundance of provisions and the profit from labor, necessarily greater in the arts than in agriculture, diverting the cultivators or their families from rustic efforts and insensibly depopulating the country, would force new settlers to be attracted from far away in order to cultivate it. Thus overburdening some points of the territory with inhabitants we would be depopulating others and, breaking the equilibrium this way, we would proceed directly against the spirit of our foundation.

Since transportation of commodities makes them more costly in factories, it will diminish the workers' profit and keeping their station closer to that of the cultivator will better maintain equilibrium between them. Nevertheless there cannot be so much of an equilibrium that the advantage will not always be for industry, either because more of the money in the state goes there, or by the means of fortune by which power and inequality play their game, or by the greater force that more men assembled have, a force which the ambitious know how to bring together for their advantage. Thus it is important that this too favored part remain in dependence upon the rest of the nation for its subsistence; in case of internal divisions it is in the nature of our foundation for the settler to give the law to the worker.

With precautions one can favor the establishment of the useful arts on the Island without danger, and I suspect that these establishments well conducted can provide for all necessary things without needing to draw anything from abroad aside from some bagatelles for which a proportionate exportation will be allowed, always carefully balanced by the administration.

To this point I have shown how the Corsican people could continue to exist comfortably and independently with very little trade, how from this little that will be necessary for it the greatest part can easily be made by exchanges, and how it can reduce the necessity for importations from outside of the Island to almost nothing. From that it is seen that if the use of money and currency cannot be absolutely annihilated in the affairs of private individuals, at least it can be reduced to so small a thing that it will be difficult for abuses to arise, that no fortunes at all will be made by this way, and that if they could be made they would become almost useless and would give little advantage to their possessors.

But how shall we govern public finances? What revenues shall we assign to the administration? Shall we establish it for free or how shall we regulate its upkeep? This is what must be considered now.

\* \* \*

Systems of finance are modern inventions. This word "finance" was no more known by the ancients than those of *taille*[18] and capitation. The word *vectigal*[19] was taken in another sense as will be said below. The sovereign laid assessments on conquered or vanquished peoples, never on its immediate subjects, above all in Republics. The people of Athens was far from being burdened with taxes, on the contrary it was paid by the Government; and Rome, whose wars must have cost so much, often made distributions of grain and even of land to the people. Nevertheless the state continued to exist, maintained large armies on sea and on land, performed considerable public works and its expenses were proportionally at least as great as those of modern states. How was this done?

Two epochs must be distinguished in States, their beginning and their growth. In the beginning of a State, it had no revenue other than the public Domain and this domain was considerable. Romulus made it one-third of all the land. He assigned the second third for the upkeep of the Priests and sacred things, only the remaining third was divided among the citizens. This was little, but this little was free. Do you believe that the French farm worker would not willingly limit himself to one third of what he cultivates on the condition of having this third free of all *taille*, of all census tax, of all tithe, and of not paying any sort of tax?

Thus the public revenue was not at all drawn in money but in produce and other commodities. The expenditure was of the same nature as the receipt. Neither the magistrates nor the troops were paid, they were fed, their clothing was provided for them, and in pressing needs extraordinary levies on the people were in statutory labor and not at all in money. These superb public labors cost the state almost nothing; they were the work of those formidable legions who worked as they fought and which were made up not of rabble but of citizens.

When the Romans began to expand and became conquerors they imposed the maintenance of their troops on the vanquished peoples, when they paid them, the subjects were taxed, never the Romans. In pressing dangers the Senate assessed itself, it took loans which it paid back faithfully and during the whole duration of the republic I do not know that the Roman people ever paid any pecuniary tax either by capitation or upon land.

Corsicans, this is a fine model! Do not be surprised that there was more virtue among the Romans than elsewhere, money was less necessary there. The State had small revenues and did great things. Its treasure was in the citizens' hands. I could say that from Corsica's situation and the form of its government there will not be a less expensive state in the world, since being an Island and a Republic it will have no need of regular troops and since the leaders of the State all return to equality they will not be able to draw anything from the common mass that does not return there in very little time.

But this is not how I envisage the nerve of the public force. On the contrary, I want much to be spent for the service of the state; to say it better I dispute only about the choice of specie. I look at finances as the fat of the body politic which, becoming congested in certain muscular webs, overburdens the body with a useless stoutness and makes it heavy rather than strong. I want to nourish the state with a healthier food which unites itself with the substance, which changes itself into fibers, into muscles without congesting the vessels, which gives vigor and not thickness to the members and which reinforces the body without weighing it down.

Far from wanting the state to be poor, on the contrary, I would like it to have everything and everyone to have his part of the common possession only in proportion to his services. The acquisition of all of the Egyptians' goods for the King done by Joseph would have been good if he had not done too much or too little.[20] But without entering into these speculations, which would take me too far away from my object, this is enough to make my thought understood, which is not to destroy private property absolutely, because that is impossible, but to restrict it within the narrowest limits, to give a measure, a rule, a brake that restrains it, that directs it, that subjugates it, and keeps it always subordinated to the public good. In a word, I want the property of the state to be as great, as strong and that of the citizens as small, as weak as possible. That is why I avoid putting it in things whose private possessor is too much the master such as currency and money that one easily hides from public inspection.

The establishment of a public domain is not, I agree, as easy a thing to do today in Corsica, already divided up among its inhabitants, as it was in nascent Rome before its conquered territory belonged to anyone. Nevertheless, I know that there remains on the Island a large quantity of excellent fallow land of which it is very easy for the government to take advantage, either by alienating it for a certain number of years to those who will put it into cultivation or by having it cleared by statutory labor in the community of each. It would be necessary to have been on the spot to judge the distribution that one could make of this land and of the advantage one can draw from it, but I do not doubt at all that by means of some exchanges and certain not very difficult arrangements one could, in each jurisdiction and even each County, procure communal estates that will even be able to increase in a few years by the order that will be spoken about in the law of inheritance.

Another means, easier still, and which ought to provide a more definite, more certain, and much more considerable revenue is to follow an example that I have under my eyes in the Protestant Cantons. Since the reformation of these Cantons, they took possession of the ecclesiastical tithes and these tithes upon which they maintain their clergy decently have made up the principal revenue of the State. I do not say that the Corsicans ought to touch the revenues of the Church, God forbid! but I believe that the people will not be extremely vexed if the State asks them for as much as the clergy—already sufficiently endowed with estates of land—ask them. The basis of this tax will be [established] without difficulty, without trouble and almost without expenses because it will only be necessary to double the ecclesiastical tithe and take half of it.

I draw a third sort of revenue, the most reliable and the best, from the men themselves, by using their labor, their arms, and their heart, rather than their purse in the service of the fatherland, either for its defense in the militias, or for its conveniences by statutory labor in public works.

Do not let this word of statutory labor be at all shocking to Republicans! I know that it is abhorred in France but is it in Switzerland? There the roads are also built by statutory labor and no one complains. The apparent convenience of payment can seduce only superficial minds and it is a reliable maxim that the fewer intermediaries there are between the need and the service, the less onerous the service ought to be.

Without daring to unfold my thought completely, without giving statutory labor and all personal work by the citizens as an absolute good here I will agree, if it is wished, that it would be better for everything to be done by paying if the means for paying did not introduce an infinite number of abuses without measure and of greater, more unlimited evils than the ones that can result from this constraint, above all if the one who imposes it is of the same station as those who are imposed upon.

Moreover, for the contribution to be divided equally it is just for the one who has no land at all and is not able to pay the tithe on its produce to pay it with the labor of his arms. Thus statutory labor ought to fall especially on the order of the aspirants. But citizens and patriots ought to lead them to labor and set the example for them. Let everything done for the public good always be honorable! Let the magistrate himself, occupied by other cares, show that those are not beneath him, like those Roman Consuls who put their hand first to the labors of the camp in order to set the example for their troops.

As to fines and confiscations which make up a fourth sort of receipt in Republics, I hope by means of the present establishment that it will be almost nothing in ours, thus I do not take it into account.

Since all these public revenues are in kind rather than in money, they appear troublesome to collect, to take care of, and to use; and that is true in part, but here it is less a question of the easiest administration than of the healthiest, and it would be better for it to give a little more trouble and to engender fewer abuses. The best economic system for Corsica and for a Republic is assuredly not the best for a monarchy and for a large state. The one that I am proposing would not succeed either in France or in England and could not even be established there, but it has the greatest success in Switzerland where it has been established for centuries, and it is the only one that it could put up with.

The receipts of each jurisdiction are farmed out; they are made in kind or in money at the choice of the contributors; the payment of the magistrates and officials is also made for the greatest part in wheat, in wine, in fodder, in wood. In this way the collection is neither troublesome for the public nor onerous to private individuals but the inconvenience that I see in it is that there are men whose profession is to make a profit from the prince and to vex the subjects.

It is extremely important in the republic not to allow financiers by station: less because of their dishonest gains than because of their principles and their examples which, too quick in spreading among the nation, destroy all good feelings from esteem for illicit abundance and its advantages, cover disinterestedness, simplicity of morals and all the virtues with disdain and opprobrium.

Let us beware of increasing the pecuniary treasury at the expense of the moral treasury; it is this latter that genuinely puts us in possession of men and of all their power, whereas by the other one obtains only the appearance of services but the will is not bought at all. It would be better for the fiscal administration to be that of the father of a family and lose something than to gain more and be that of a usurer.

Let us leave tax collection in state control, even if it must bring in much less. Let us even avoid making this tax collection into a profession, for this would be almost the same inconvenience as farming it out. What makes a system of finance most pernicious is the use of a financier. Whatever the price might be, there must be no publicans in the state. Instead of making tax collection and public revenues a lucrative profession, on the contrary, it is necessary to make it the test of the merit and integrity of young citizens; it is necessary for this tax collection to be, so to speak, the novitiate of public employment and the first step toward attaining magistracies. What suggested this idea to me is the comparison of the administration of the Charity Hospital of Paris whose depredations and acts of brigandage are known to everyone, with the Charity Hospital of Lyon which offers an example of order and disinterestedness which perhaps has no equal on earth. Where does this difference come from? Are the Lyonnais in themselves worth more than the Parisians? No. But at Lyon this office of administration is a station of passage. It is necessary to begin by filling it well in order to be able to become Alderman and Provost of merchants while at Paris the administrators are such by station for their whole life; they contrive to draw the best possible advantage from an employment that is not a test for them but a profession, a reward, a station attached, so to speak, to other stations. There are certain positions about which it is agreed that the revenues will be increased by the right to rob the poor.

And do not think that this labor requires more experience and enlightenment than young people can have; it requires only a level of activity for which they are singularly suited, and since they are ordinarily less avaricious, less harsh in exactions than old people are, being on the one side sensitive to the miseries of the poor and on the other strongly interested in filling well an employment that serves as a test for them, they behave precisely as befits the thing.

The receiver of each parish will render his accounts to his county, that of each county to its jurisdiction, and that of each jurisdiction to the chamber of accounts which will be composed of a certain number of councillors of State and presided over by the Doge. In this manner, the public treasury will consist for the most part in commodities and other products divided into small warehouses over the whole kingdom and for some part in money that will be put into the general coffer after small expenses to make on the spot have been withdrawn.

Since private individuals will always be free to pay their quota in money or in produce at the levels that will be set every year in each jurisdiction, once the government has calculated the best proportion that ought to be found between these two sorts of quotas, as soon as this proportion is altered it will be in a position to notice this alteration on the spot, to seek its cause and to remedy it.

This is the key to our political Government, the only part that requires art, calculations, meditation. This is why the chamber of accounts, which everywhere else is only a very subordinate tribunal, will be the center of business here, will give the impetus to the whole administration and will be composed of the foremost heads of the state.

When collections in produce go beyond their measure and those in money do not reach theirs, this will be a sign that agriculture and population are going well, but that useful industry is being neglected; it will be appropriate to rekindle it a bit out of fear that the private individuals, having also become too isolated, too independent, too unsociable will not hold the government highly enough.

But this defect of proportion, an infallible sign of prosperity, will always be little to be feared and easy to remedy. It will not be the same for the contrary defect which, as soon as it makes itself felt, is already of the greatest consequence and cannot be corrected too early. For when the contributors provide more money than commodities this will be a certain mark that there is too much exportation to foreign countries, that commerce is becoming too easy, that the lucrative arts are being extended on the Island at the expense of agriculture and consequently that simplicity and all the virtues attached to it are beginning to degenerate. The abuses that produce this alteration indicate the remedies that must be brought to it, but these remedies require a great wisdom in the manner of administering them; for here it is easier to prevent the evil than to destroy it.

If one did nothing but put taxes on the objects of luxury, close one's ports to foreign commerce, suppress manufacturing, stop the circulation of specie, one would do nothing but throw the people into laziness, misery, discouragement; one will make money disappear without increasing produce; one will remove the resource of fortune without reestablishing that of labor. To touch the value of currencies is also a bad operation in a republic, first because then the public robs itself which signifies nothing at all, in the second place because, between the quantity of signs and that of things, there is a proportion that always regulates their respective value in the same way and because when the Prince wants to change the signs he does nothing but change the names since then the value of the things necessarily changes in the same relation. Among Kings it is a different matter and when the Prince inflates the currency he draws the real advantage from it of robbing his creditors: but if this operation is ever repeated this advantage is neutralized and erased by the loss of public credit.

Establish sumptuary laws, then, but make them always more severe for the foremost people in the State, relax them for the inferior orders;

act so that there is vanity in being simple and so that a rich person does not know how to make himself honored for his money. These are not impractical speculations at all: this is how the Venetians grant only to their nobles the right of wearing their coarse ugly cloth from Padua, so that the best city-dwellers hold it an honor to have the same permission.

When there is simplicity in morals, agrarian laws are necessary, because then the rich man, not being able to place his wealth in anything else, accumulates his possessions: but neither[21] agrarian laws nor any laws can ever have a retroactive effect and one cannot confiscate any land acquired legitimately however large it might be in virtue of a posterior law that forbids having that much.

No law can despoil any private individual of any portion of his possession. Law can only keep him from acquiring more; then if he breaks the law he deserves punishment and the illegitimately acquired surplus ought to be confiscated. The Romans saw the necessity of agrarian laws when it was no longer time to establish them, and, for lack of the distinction I have just made, they finally destroyed the Republic by a means that ought to have preserved it: the Gracchi[22] wanted to deprive the Patricians of their lands; it would have been necessary to prevent them from acquiring them. It is very true that afterwards these same Patricians acquired more in spite of the law, but this is because the evil was deep-rooted when it was passed and it was too late to remedy it.

Fear and hope are the two instruments with which one governs men; but instead of using the one and the other indiscriminately, it is necessary to use them in accordance with their nature. Fear does not excite, it holds back; and its use in penal laws is not to lead people to do good but to keep them from doing evil. We do not even see that fear of poverty makes idle people laborious. Thus in order to excite among men a genuine emulation in labor one must not show it to them as a means for avoiding hunger but as a means of proceeding to well-being. Thus let us posit this general rule that no one ought to be castigated for having abstained but for having acted.

Thus in order to awaken a nation's activity it is necessary to give it great desires, great hopes, great positive motives for acting.[23] When well examined, the great motive powers that make men act are reduced to two, sensual pleasure and vanity, still if you remove from the first everything that belongs to the second, in the final analysis, you will find that everything is reduced almost to vanity alone. It is easy to see that all those who show off their pursuit of sensual pleasure are merely vain. Their so-called sensual pleasure is merely ostentation, it consists more in showing it or describing it than in tasting it. True pleasure is simple and peaceful, it

loves silence and introspection; the one who tastes it belongs completely
to the thing, he does not amuse himself by saying, "I am having some
pleasure." Now vanity is the fruit of opinion; it is born from it and nour-
ishes itself upon it. From which it follows that the arbiters of a people's
opinion are the arbiters of its actions. It seeks things in proportion to the
value it gives them; to show it what it ought to esteem is to tell it what it
ought to do.

This name, vanity, is not well chosen because it is only one of the two
branches of amour-propre. I must explain myself. The opinion that puts
a great value on frivolous objects produces vanity; the one that falls upon
objects great and beautiful by themselves produces pride. One can thus
make a people prideful or vain according to the selection of the objects
upon which one directs its judgments.

Pride is more natural than vanity because it consists in esteeming
oneself based on truly estimable goods, whereas vanity, giving a value to
what does not have any at all is the work of prejudices slow to be born.
Some time is necessary to fascinate a nation's eyes. Since there is nothing
more really beautiful than independence and power, at first every people
that is formed is prideful. But no new people was ever vain, because by
its nature vanity is individual; it cannot be the instrument of such a great
thing as forming the body of a nation.[24]

Two contrary states cast men into the torpor of laziness. One is that
peace of soul that makes one satisfied with what one possesses; the other
an insatiable longing that makes one feel the impossibility of satisfying
it. The one who lives without desires and the one who knows he cannot
obtain what he desires remain equally in inaction. In order to act one
must both aspire to something and be able to hope to attain it. Every
government that wants to make the people active ought to take care to
put into its grasp objects capable of tempting it. Make it so that labor
offers great advantages to citizens, not only according to your estimation
but according to theirs; you will infallibly make them laborious.[25] Among
these advantages, not only is wealth not always the most attractive, but it
can be less so than any other, as long as it does not serve as a means for
attaining the ones by which one is tempted.

The most general and the surest way that one can have for satisfying
one's desires, whatever they might be, is power. Thus toward whatever
passion a man or a people might be inclined, if he has some lively ones he
avidly aspires to power, either as an end if he is prideful or vain, or as a
means if he is vindictive or a lover of pleasure.

Thus the great art of government consists in the economy of civil
power well understood, not only in order to maintain it, but in order to

diffuse activity and life into the whole state; in order to make the people active and laborious.

Civil power is exercised in two manners: the one legitimate from authority, the other abusive from wealth. Everywhere that wealth dominates, power and authority are ordinarily separated, because the means of acquiring wealth and the means of attaining authority, not being the same, are rarely employed by the same people. Then the apparent power is in the hands of the magistrates and the real power is in those of the rich. In such a government everything proceeds at the pleasure of men, nothing tends toward the goal of the foundation.

It happens then that the object of longing is divided: some aspire to authority in order to sell its use to the rich and to enrich themselves by this means; the others and the greatest number go directly toward wealth with which they are sure of having power one day by buying either authority or those who are its depositaries.

Assume that, in a State constituted this way, on the one side, honors and authority are hereditary, and that, on the other, the means of acquiring wealth are within the grasp of a small number and depend on influence, favor, friends; then it is impossible, while some adventurers proceed to fortune and from there by degrees to positions, for a universal discouragement not to reach the bulk of the nation and not to cast it into languor.

# Separate Fragments

Thus generally in every rich nation the government is weak, I call by this name equally the one that acts only weakly and, what amounts to the same, the one that needs violent means to maintain itself.

I cannot clarify my thought any better than by the example of Carthage and Rome. The first massacred, crucified its generals, its magistrates, its members and was only a weak government that everything incessantly frightened and shook. The second deprived no one of his life, did not even confiscate possessions, the accused criminal could leave it peacefully and the trial ended there. The vigor of this admirable government did not need cruelty; the greatest of misfortunes was to cease to be one of its members.

Peoples will be laborious when labor is held in honor and it always depends on the government to make it so. Let consideration and authority be in the grasp of the Citizens, they will exert themselves to reach them; but if they see them as too far away they will not make a step. What casts them into discouragement is not the amount of the labor, it is its uselessness.

I will be asked if it is while plowing one's field that one acquires the talents necessary for governing. I will answer, yes in a simple and upright government such as ours. Great talents are the supplement of patriotic zeal, they are necessary for leading a people that does not love its country at all and does not honor its leaders at all. But act so that the people delight in the commonwealth, look for virtues and leave your great talents; they would do more harm than good. The best motive force of a government is love of the fatherland and this love is cultivated along with the fields. Good sense is enough to lead a well constituted state, and good sense is elaborated as much in the heart as in the head, men whose passions do not blind them always act well.

Men are naturally lazy but the ardor for labor is the first fruit of a well-regulated society and when a people falls back into laziness and discouragement it is always from the abuse of this same society that no longer gives to labor the value it ought to expect.

Everywhere money reigns that which the people gives in order to maintain its freedom is always the instrument of its slavery and what it pays voluntarily today is used to make it pay by force tomorrow.

Every child born on the Island will be a citizen and member of the Republic when he is old enough according to the statutes, and none will be able to be one except in this manner.

Thus it will not be possible to give the right of the city to any foreigner aside from one single time every fifty years to a single one if he presents himself and if he is judged worthy of it, or the most worthy of those who present themselves. His reception will be a general festival on the whole Island.

Every Corsican who, having reached forty years of age, is not married and has not been so at all will be excluded from the right of the City for his whole life.

Every private individual who, changing residence, passes from one county to another will lose his right of the City for three years and at the end of this time will be inscribed in the new county upon paying a fee, without which he will continue to be excluded from the right of the City until he has paid.

From the preceding point are excepted all those who fill any public charge who ought to be admitted to all the rights of the City in the county in which they are found as long as they are in office.

The Corsicans were subject to the Genoese. It is known what treatment forced them to revolt, almost forty years ago. Since that time they have kept themselves independent. Nevertheless the Gazetteers always call them rebels and it is not known for how many centuries they will continue to call them thus. The present generation has not seen servitude at all: it is hard to conceive how a man born free and who keeps himself such is a rebel while a lucky usurper is a sacred monarch, a legitimate King at the end of three years. Thus prescription takes place only in favor of Tyranny, it is never allowed in favor of freedom. This sentiment is as reasonable in itself as it is honorable to its partisans. Fortunately words are not things. Ransomed at the price of their blood, the Corsicans, rebels or not, are free and worthy of being so in spite of the Genoese and the Gazetteers.

In each county will be kept a register of all the land that each private individual possesses.

None will be able to possess land outside of his county.

None will be able to possess more than [ ]²⁶ land. One who has this quantity will be able to acquire similar quantities by exchange, but not larger ones even of less good land and all gifts, all legacies that could be given to him in land will be nullified.

Because you have governed a free people justly for three years, it entrusts the same administration to you for three more years.

No bachelor will be able to make a will, but all his possessions will pass to the community.

Corsicans, keep silence, I am going to speak in the name of all. Let those who will not consent go away, and let those who will consent raise their hand.

It will be necessary to have this act preceded by a general proclamation bringing an injunction to each to make his way to the place of his residence at a time that will be prescribed, under pain of losing his right of birth and naturalization.

# I

The whole Corsican nation will combine by a solemn oath into a single body politic of which both the bodies that compose it and the individuals will be members henceforth.

# II

This act of union will be celebrated the same day on the whole Island and all Corsicans will attend it to the best of their ability, each in his city, village, or parish as will be more specifically ordered.

# III

Formula of the oath pronounced under the sky and hand on the Bible:

In the name of omnipotent God and upon the holy Gospels by a sacred and irrevocable oath I unite myself by body, by possessions, by will, and by all my power to the Corsican nation in order to belong to it in all property, myself and all that depends on me. I swear to live and die for it, to observe all its laws and to obey its legitimate leaders and magistrates in everything that is in conformity to the laws. Thus may God help me in this life and have mercy on my soul. May freedom, justice, and the Republic of the Corsicans live forever. Amen.

And all keeping the right hand raised will answer: Amen.

In each parish there will be kept a precise register of all those who have assisted in this solemnity. Their name, their father's name, their age and their residence will be noted in it.

As for those who will not have been able to assist at this solemnity for valid impediment other days will be assigned to swear the same oath and have themselves inscribed in the space of three months at the latest after the solemn oath; when this term has passed all those who have neglected to fulfill this duty will have their right foreclosed, and will remain in the Class of foreigners or aspirants which will be spoken about below.

A country has its greatest independent force when the land there produces as much as possible, that is, when it has as many cultivators as it wants.

For each child he has of more than five years of age he will be allotted a *patrimony* on the township.

Fathers who have children who are absent will not be able to have them go through the accounting until after their return and those who are off the Island for an entire year will no longer be able to be counted even after their return.

They will be turned away from superstition by being very much occupied with their duties as citizens; by having display put into national festivals, by having much of their time taken away from ecclesiastical ceremonies in order to give them to civil ceremonies, and that can be done with a little skill without making the Clergy angry, by acting so that it always has some share in them, but so that this share is so small that attention does not stay fixed on them at all.

Of all manners of living the one that attaches men most to their country is the rustic life.

The Guardians of the Laws will be able to convoke the estates general whenever they want and, from the day of convocation to the day after the assembly, the authority of the great Podesta and of the council of state will be suspended.

The person of the guardians of the laws will be sacred and inviolable and there will be no one on the Island who has the power to arrest them.

Each County will have the right to revoke its guardians and of substituting others for them whenever it pleases but unless they are expressly recalled they will be for life.

Once convoked extraordinarily by the Senate, the Estates will not be able to be dissolved unless the Senate or the great Podesta are dismissed.

The Laws concerning inheritances ought all to tend to bring things back to equality so that each might have something and no one have anything in excess.

Every Corsican who leaves his county in order to go to live in another will lose his right of the city for three years. At the end of which upon his request and a proclamation, if no charge is brought against him, he will be inscribed on the registers of the new county and in the same order into which he was inscribed in the other: citizen if he was citizen and patriot if he was patriot and aspirant if he was only an aspirant.

And Corsicans must pay a duty in order to obtain the favor of being unarmed.

There will be no carriages on the Island; Ecclesiastics and women will be able to make use of two-wheeled chaises. But laymen of any rank whatsoever will be able to travel only on foot or on horseback unless they are crippled or seriously ill.

None will be allowed to take an oath on things concerning his interest. But the oath . . .

None will be able to be put in prison for debt and even in seizures that might be made in the house of a debtor, he will be left with (in addition to clothes to cover himself) his plow, his oxen, his bed and his most indispensable furnishings.

Every boy who gets married before having reached the age of twenty or only after having reached the age of thirty, or who marries a girl who has not reached the age of fifteen, or a person—maid or widow—whose age differs from his by more than twenty years will remain excluded from the order of citizens until he attains it by public reward for services rendered to the State.

Given the unequal distribution of the productions of the Island it is necessary not to close communications; in some things it is necessary to have consideration for the people's prejudice and shortsightedness. Seeing that one does not allow it to go to its neighborhood to seek among its compatriots the commodities it lacks, it would accuse our laws of capriciousness and of harshness, it would mutiny against them, or would hate them in secret.

If we could do without money and have all the advantages that money gives we would enjoy these advantages much better than we would with wealth, because we would have them separated from the vices that poison them and that money brings along with it.

None ought to be magistrate by station nor soldier by station. All ought to be ready to fill the functions the fatherland imposes on them indiscriminately. There ought not to be any permanent station on the Island other than that of citizen and that one alone ought to comprehend all the others.

As long as money is useful to the Corsicans they will love it, and as long as they love it the Republic will maintain among them emissaries and treaties that will have influence over deliberations and, so to speak, will keep the State in the pay of its former masters.

One must not at all count on a lively but always brief enthusiasm after freedom is recovered. Popular Heroism is a moment of fire that follows languor and slackening. It is necessary to found a people's freedom upon its manner of being and not on its passions. For the passions are temporary and change their object; but the effect of a good constitution lasts as long as the constitution and no people could remain free except for as long as it feels well as a result of freedom.

May they remember well that every sort of privilege is for the profit of the private individuals who obtain them and the burden of the nation that gives them.

This is the ridiculous contradiction into which fall all violent governments that, wanting to keep peoples in a condition of weakness nevertheless want to put themselves into a condition of strength from them.

The nation will not be at all illustrious but it will be happy. It will not be spoken about; it will have little consideration abroad; but it will have abundance, peace, and freedom in its bosom.

Every litigant who has rejected the arbitration of the elders or who, having accepted it refuses to rely on their judgment if he loses his suit in law court, will be noted down and unable to exercise any public employment for five years.

Every daughter of a citizen who marries a Corsican of any class whatsoever will be given a dowry by the husband's county; this dowry will always be a piece of land and, if he is an aspirant, will suffice for him to ascend to the class of patriots.

Of all governments the Democratic is always the least expensive because public luxury is only in the abundance of men, and because, where the people is the master, power has no need of any dazzling sign.

For two or several States to be subject to the same Prince, that has nothing contrary to right or to reason. But that a State be subject to another State, that appears incompatible with the nature of the body politic.

Although I know the Corsican nation has prejudices very contrary to my principles, my intention is not at all to employ the art of persuading in order to make them adopt them. On the contrary I want to tell them my opinion and my reasons with such simplicity that there is nothing in it that can seduce them, because it is very possible that I am mistaken and I would be very sorry for them to adopt my sentiment to their harm.

From where do the dissensions, quarrels, civil wars come in Corsica that have torn it apart for so many years and finally forced it to have recourse to the Pisans, then to the Genoese? Isn't all that the work of its nobility, isn't it the nobility that reduced the people to despair and forced it to prefer a tranquil slavery to the ills that it was suffering under so many Tyrants? Now after having shaken off the yoke does it want to return into the state that forced it to submit to it?

I shall not preach morality to them,[27] I shall not order them to have virtues, but I shall put them in a position so that they will have virtues without knowing the word; and so that they will be good and just without knowing very well what justice and goodness are.

I do not know how it happens, but I do know very well that the operations for which one keeps the most registers and account books are precisely those in which the most knavery is committed.

Such were the young Romans who began by being questors or treasurers of arms before commanding them. Such financiers were not base men, it did not even enter into their heads that one could profit from public money, and military cash boxes could pass into the hands of the Catos without risk.

Instead of [repressing] luxury by means of sumptuary laws, it would be better to forestall it by an administration that makes it impossible.

I am persuaded that by looking for them well one will find iron mines on the Island; it would be better to find iron mines there than gold mines.

And in doubt itself it is better to begin by the state that naturally leads to the other and which one can always do without if one hopes to find a better one, than by the one from which one cannot not return to the other, and which has nothing before it but destruction and ruin.

*Le prerogative che godernno le sudette famiglie.*[28]

This point is destructive of the spirit of the Republic which wants the military to be extremely subordinated to the magistrate and regards itself only as the minister of the ministers of the law. It is extremely important that the military not be a station by itself, but an accident of the station of citizen. If the nobility had prerogatives, distinctions in the Troops, soon military officers would believe they were above civil officials; the leaders of the Republic would no longer be regarded as anything but Men of the Robe,[29] and being governed militarily the state would very promptly fall under despotism.

To see the man who has been so much respected while he is in place return to the private station is an excellent means of teaching how to relate everything to the law, and for him to be assured that one day he will find himself back again in their number is a great lesson for maintaining the rights of private individuals.

For example, since the province of Capo Corso is unable to produce anything but wine, it is necessary that there not be enough cultivated in all the rest of the Island so that this part cannot sell its own.

For since private property is so weak and so dependent, the Government needs only a little force and, so to speak, leads the people with a movement of its finger.

Where are the Princes who take it into their head to assemble Theologians in order to consult whether what they want to undertake is legitimate?

## Preface

I have a profound respect for the Republic of Genoa; I have one for every sovereign in particular, even though I sometimes tell all of them truths that are a little harsh. And would heaven grant for their own advantage that one might dare to tell them to them more often and that they sometimes might deign to listen to them.

Pay attention I beg you to the fact that I am not giving statutory labor or any sort of forced labor as an absolute good; it would be better for all that to be done freely and by paying, if the means of paying did not introduce an infinity of abuses without measure of greater evils, more unlimited than those that can result from this constraint above all when those who impose it are of the same station as those who are imposed upon.

For if there is only one sort of revenue, namely the fruits of the earth, there will be no more than one sort of possession, namely the earth itself.

For the genuine spirit of public property is that for private property to be very strong in the stock and very weak or nonexistent in the collateral.

And to raise the taxes in order to give value to the commodity and to take value away from money.

The Corsicans are almost still in the natural and healthy state, but much art is needed to keep them there because their prejudices are taking them away from it, they have precisely what suits them but they want what is not good for them; their sentiments are upright, it is their false enlightenment that fools them. They see the false glitter of neighboring nations and burn to be like them, because they do not feel their misery and do not see that they are infinitely better.

To prevent the exportation of commodities is to cut off the great holdings by the root.

Noble people, I do not at all want to give you artificial and systematic laws invented by men but to lead you back underneath the laws of nature and of order alone which command hearts and do not tyrannize wills at all.

1. Rousseau originally began, "If the Island of Corsica were entirely free and subject to its inhabitants alone, it could take advantage of its situation and of its advantages to put itself into a flourishing state and, following the example of the other powers of Italy, to form establishments which by industry, navy, and commerce, would make it cut a figure abroad."

2. In one of the manuscripts Rousseau added the following as a note: "The Barbary pirates hardly harass the Corsicans at present because they know that there is nothing to gain with them, but as soon as the latter begin to carry on commerce and the exchange of merchandise they will rage. You will have them on your hands."

3. Rousseau originally wrote, "The force of wealth (greatness) in the State consists solely in the number of its peoples. Money itself is only a means for having men."

4. This memorandum was written by Mathieu Buttafoco who asked Rousseau to write this *Plan*.

5. The term translated as "county" is *pièves*.

6. In another version of this passage Rousseau wrote, "You should not hesitate at all to finish their work; while believing they are working for themselves they will be working for you. The means are the same only the end is very different: for that of the Genoese was to debase the nobility and ours is to ennoble the nation."

7. It was the Treaty of Aix-la-Chapelle that put Corsica under Genoese control in 1748.

8. Land belonging to the community.

9. On this side and on that side of the mountains.

10. After this paragraph Rousseau originally wrote, "In order to arrive at this it is first necessary to know the national character of the people to govern and if it did not have one it would be necessary to give it one. Every man who does not wear, so to speak, the livery of his country in his soul cannot be a good citizen or a faithful subject and legislation does not consist in what all the laws in the world have in common, but in what they have that is different."

11. This passage is from Terrasson's translation of the *Universal History* by Diodorus Siculus.

12. In the manuscript, the footnote that occurs here comes after this paragraph. It is accompanied by the remark, "NB to place."

13. In one of the manuscripts Rousseau wrote and crossed out, "Let us now see by what means one can render this fatal sign less necessary without harming. . . . The need of minted specie increases or decreases in a state to the extent that exchange becomes more or [less] necessary and government becomes more or less expensive. Thus without (commerce and without finances) business, private individuals would have no need of money and without public finances the State would not have any need for it either. (If private individuals had no business they would have no need for money. Remove business and exchanges, private individuals would have no need . . .)"

14. Rousseau first wrote, "Since no one (being able then) has any other interest in the trade of commodities from one province to another so that the necessities of these trades are always proportional to the need."

15. Reading "décourage" instead of "dérourage," which is found in Pléiade, III, 925.

16. Rousseau originally added here, "Since real abundance is the sole object of luxury, each will seek to distinguish himself by that luxury."

17. Rousseau was living at Môtiers at the time.

18. On *taille*, see n. 140, p. 25 above.

19. The vectigal was a payment of tribute.

20. For the story of Joseph, see *Genesis* 37:1.

21. Reading "ni" instead of "si" as in Pléiade, III, 916.

22. In the second century B.C. the Gracchi brothers sponsored controversial agrarian laws in Rome.

23. In the manuscript the following sentence follows but is crossed out, "They have never been able to make savages work because they do not desire anything. Europeans have never been able to attract them to their manner of living because they attach no importance to it."

24. Between this paragraph and the next one Rousseau wrote and circled the following, "from this mutual dependence which one believe to the bond of society is born all the vices that destroy it. —The English people does not love freedom by itself; it loves it because it produces money."

25. At this point in the manuscript occurs the following passage, circled, "It is then that it will be necessary to use the surplus on industry and the arts in order to attract from the foreigner what such a large people lacks for its subsistence. Also then will be born little by little the vices inseparable from these establishments and which—by degrees corrupting the nation in its tastes and in its principles—will finally corrupt and destroy the government. This evil is inevitable and since all human things must come to an end; it is fine that after a long and vigorous existence a state finish by excess of population."

26. Rousseau left a blank space where the amount would be.

27. Rousseau originally added, "because sermons do not make anyone act."

28. This quotation is the beginning of a proposal to reestablish the Corsican nobility.

29. The term used here is *Robins,* which has a derogatory connotation.